ALBERT ELISHA

AND THEY ALL BEGAN TO SPEAK IN OTHER TONGUES

Speaking in Tongues Is an Accompanying Sign, It Is Supernatural, and It Is for All—Yes, You Too!

In this book, the terms
- 'Speaking in tongues,'
- 'Praying in tongues,'
- 'Praying with the Spirit,' and
- 'Praying in the [Holy] Spirit.'
all mean the same.

SPEAKING IN TONGUES IS FOR ALL.

THESE ARE Paul's words.

He says to the church in Corinth,

> [1 Corinthians 14:18]
> *I thank my God, I SPEAK WITH TONGUES MORE THAN YE ALL ...*

Does this mean that all members of the church in Corinth spoke in tongues?

All—as in *everyone*?

Yes.

In Mark 16, Jesus said that speaking in tongues is a sign that follows all who believe.

> [Mark 16:15-20]
> *15 And he [Jesus] said unto them, Go ye into all the world, and preach the gospel to every creature.*
> *16 He that believeth and is baptized shall be saved; but he that believeth not shall be damned.*
> *17 And THESE SIGNS SHALL SHALL*

5

FOLLOW THEM THAT BELIEVE; In my name shall they cast out devils; THEY SHALL SPEAK WITH NEW TONGUES;

18 They shall take up serpents; and if they drink any deadly thing, it shall not hurt them; they shall lay hands on the sick, and they shall recover.

19 So then after the Lord had spoken unto them, he was received up into heaven, and sat on the right hand of God.

20 And they went forth, and preached every where, the Lord working with them, and CONFIRMING THE WORD WITH SIGNS FOLLOWING. ...

We see that in the book of Acts.

We see that speaking in tongues is an accompanying sign that is present when people receive the Holy Spirit.

On the day of Pentecost, for example.

All who received the Holy Spirit on that day also spoke in tongues.

[Acts 2:1-4]

1 And when the day of Pentecost was fully come, they were all with one accord in one place.

2 And suddenly there came a sound from heaven as of a rushing mighty wind, and it filled all the house where they were sitting.

3 And there appeared unto them cloven tongues like as of fire, and it sat upon each of them.

4 And THEY WERE ALL FILLED WITH THE HOLY [SPIRIT], AND BEGAN TO SPEAK WITH OTHER TONGUES, AS THE SPIRIT GAVE THEM UTTERANCE.

This sets the standard.

That is why we also see everyone in Acts 10 receive the Holy Spirit and speak in tongues.

A whole household.

Acts 10:44:47]

44 While Peter yet spake these words, THE HOLY [SPIRIT] FELL ON ALL THEM WHICH HEARD THE WORD.

45 And they of the circumcision which believed were astonished, as many as came with Peter, because that on the Gentiles also was poured out the gift of the Holy [Spirit].

46 FOR THEY HEARD THEM SPEAK WITH TONGUES and magnify God.

> *Then answered Peter, 47 Can any man forbid water, that these should not be baptized, which HAVE RECEIVED THE HOLY [SPIRIT] AS WELL AS WE?*

We also see the disciples in Ephesus in Acts 19 receive the Holy Spirit, and all speak in tongues.

> [Acts 19:5-6]
>
> *5 When they heard this, they were baptized in the name of the Lord Jesus.*
> *6 And when Paul had laid his hands upon them, THE HOLY [SPIRIT] CAME ON THEM; AND THEY SPAKE WITH TONGUES, and prophesied.*

In the letters of the apostles, we also see that all the believers also spoke in tongues.

As we've said, Paul said to the Corinthians,

> [1 Corinthians 14:18]
>
> *I thank my God, I SPEAK WITH TONGUES MORE THAN YE ALL ...*

But not just all the members of the church in Corinthian spoke in tongues.

All the members of the other churches spoke in tongues as well.

That's what we can glean from the letters of the apostles.

In Romans, Paul talks about how the Holy Spirit helps us when we pray in tongues.

[Romans 8:26-28]

26 Likewise THE SPIRIT ALSO HELPETH OUR INFIRMITIES: FOR WE KNOW NOT WHAT WE SHOULD PRAY FOR AS WE OUGHT: BUT THE SPIRIT ITSELF MAKETH INTERCESSION FOR US WITH GROANINGS WHICH CANNOT BE UTTERED.

27 And he that searcheth the hearts knoweth what is the mind of the Spirit, because he maketh intercession for the saints according to the will of God.

28 And we know that all things work together for good to them that love God, to them who are the called according to his purpose.

In 1st Corinthians, Paul talks much about speaking in tongues and spiritual gifts. See 1 Corinthians chapters 12-14

In Ephesians, Paul instructs the Ephesian believers to pray in tongues at all times.

10 Finally, my brethren, be strong in the Lord, and in the power of his might.

11 Put on the whole armour of God, that ye may be able to stand against the wiles of the devil.

12 For we wrestle not against flesh and blood, but against principalities, against powers, against the rulers of the darkness of this world, against spiritual wickedness in high places.

13 Wherefore take unto you the whole armour of God, that ye may be able to withstand in the evil day, and having done all, to stand.

14 Stand therefore, having your loins girt about with truth, and having on the breastplate of righteousness;

15 And your feet shod with the preparation of the gospel of peace;

16 Above all, taking the shield of faith, wherewith ye shall be able to quench all the fiery darts of the wicked.

17 And take the helmet of salvation, and the sword of the Spirit, which is the word of God:

18 PRAYING ALWAYS WITH ALL PRAYER AND SUPPLICATION IN THE SPIRIT, and watching thereunto with all perseverance and supplication for all saints ...

In his letter, Jude instructs the believers to build themselves up by praying in tongues.

[Jude 17-21]

17 But, beloved, remember ye the words which were spoken before of the apostles of our Lord Jesus Christ;

18 How that they told you there should be mockers in the last time, who should walk after their own ungodly lusts.

19 These be they who separate themselves, sensual, HAVING NOT THE SPIRIT.

20 But ye, BELOVED, BUILDING UP YOURSELVES ON YOUR MOST HOLY FAITH, PRAYING IN THE HOLY [SPIRIT],

21 Keep yourselves in the love of God, looking for the mercy of our Lord Jesus Christ unto eternal life.

So we see that, according to the Scriptures, speaking in tongues is for all.

And these SIGNS SHALL FOLLOW THEM THAT BELIEVE; ... THEY SHALL SPEAK WITH NEW TONGUES

...

- Mark 16:17

And they WERE ALL FILLED WITH THE HOLY [SPIRIT], AND BEGAN TO SPEAK WITH OTHER TONGUES, as the Spirit gave them utterance.

- Acts 2:4

CONTENTS

PART 1: SPEAKING IN TONGUES IS AN ACCOMPANYING SIGN

1 SPEAKING IN TONGUES IS AN ACCOMPANYING SIGN.

ACCORDING to Jesus, speaking in tongues is for all believers.

Before He ascended, Jesus said,

[Mark 16:17]

And these signs will follow THEM THAT BELIEVE: ... THEY SHALL SPEAK WITH NEW TONGUES ...

Jesus said this at the end of the book of Mark. At that time, this was not yet happening.

But once Jesus was glorified and poured out the Holy Spirit, these things are taking place: in the book of Acts.

The book of Acts is our gold standard.

In Acts, we also see that all believers received the Holy Spirit and spoke in tongues as an accompanying sign.

2 WHEN PEOPLE RECEIVE THE HOLY SPIRIT, THEY WILL ALSO SPEAK IN TONGUES.

IN THE BOOK of Acts, 4 accounts tell us precisely what happened when people received the Holy Spirit.

In 3 of those 4 accounts, they also spoke in tongues.

In Acts 2:

[Acts 2:4]

And they were all filled with the Holy [Spirit] and BEGAN TO SPEAK WITH OTHER TONGUES, as the Spirit gave them utterance.

In Acts 10:

[Acts 10:44-46]

44 While Peter yet spake these words,

the Holy [Spirit] fell on all them which heard the word.

45 And they of the circumcision which believed were astonished, as many as came with Peter, because that on the Gentiles also was poured out the gift of the Holy [Spirit].

46 For THEY HEARD THEM SPEAK WITH TONGUES, and magnify God. ...

In Acts 19:

[Acts 19:6]

And when Paul had laid his hands upon them, the Holy [Spirit] came on them; and they SPAKE WITH TONGUES, and prophesied.

In one more account, it says a bystander could see when people received the Holy Spirit.

[Acts 8:17-18]

17 Then [Peter and John] laid they their hands on them, and they received the Holy [Spirit].

18 And when Simon SAW that through laying on of the apostles' hands the Holy [Spirit] was given ...

So there must have been also an accompanying sign.

27

3 BUT THERE ARE DIFFERENT TYPES OF SPEAKING IN TONGUES.

THERE IS the accompanying sign of tongues, according to Jesus in Mark 16:

[Mark 16:17]

And these SIGNS SHALL FOLLOW them that believe: ... THEY SHALL SPEAK WITH NEW TONGUES ...

The sign of tongues is for all believers.

It is a prayer language. We can use it to build ourselves up.

[Jude 17-21]

17 But, beloved, remember ye the words which were spoken before of the apostles of our Lord Jesus Christ;

18 How that they told you there should be mockers in the last time, who should walk after their own ungodly lusts.

> *19 These be they who separate themselves, sensual, having not the Spirit.*
>
> *20 BUT YE, BELOVED, BUILDING UP YOURSELVES ON YOUR MOST HOLY FAITH, PRAYING IN THE HOLY [SPIRIT],*
>
> *21 Keep yourselves in the love of God, looking for the mercy of our Lord Jesus Christ unto eternal life.*

But there is also another type of tongues: the gift of tongues, according to Paul in 1 Corinthians 12.

> [1 Corinthians 12:8,10]
>
> *... for to one is given ... , TO ANOTHER DIVERS KINDS OF TONGUES, TO ANOTHER THE INTERPRETATION OF TONGUES.*

The gift of tongues in 1 Corinthians 12 is a gift of the Holy Spirit that the Holy Spirit distributes as He wills.

It goes together with the gift of interpretation of tongues.

So, all believers who have received the Holy Spirit speak in tongues for personal edification.

But not all believers also operate in the

gift of tongues.

I deal with this question in more detail in one of my books. See *Do All Speak in Tongues: Yes and No.*

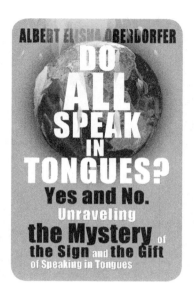

This current book, *"And They All Began to Speak in Tongues,"* only deals with the *sign* of speaking in tongues.

The kind of speaking in tongues that is for *all* believers.

PART 2: SPEAKING IN TONGUES IS SUPERNATURAL

4 SPEAKING IN TONGUES IS A SUPERNATURAL ACTIVITY.

PAUL SAYS in 1 Corinthians 14:2:

[1 Corinthians 14:2]

FOR HE THAT SPEAKETH IN AN UNKNOWN TONGUE SPEAKETH NOT UNTO MEN, BUT UNTO GOD: for no man understandeth him; howbeit, IN THE SPIRIT HE SPEAKETH MYSTERIES.

The word "mysteries" means hidden truths.

So when we speak in tongues, we speak divine hidden truths.

When we speak a known language, we communicate with other people. In that case, our mind is heavily involved. Because before we can speak a known language, we need to have learned it.

But when we speak in tongues, we don't speak to other people. We speak to God. We don't understand the language, and others don't understand it either.

Because when we speak in tongues, we speak in the spirit. So only our spirit is involved—not our mind.

That is why speaking in tongues will offend the mind. Because our mind is so used to running the show of our lives. But when we speak in tongues, the mind is left out.

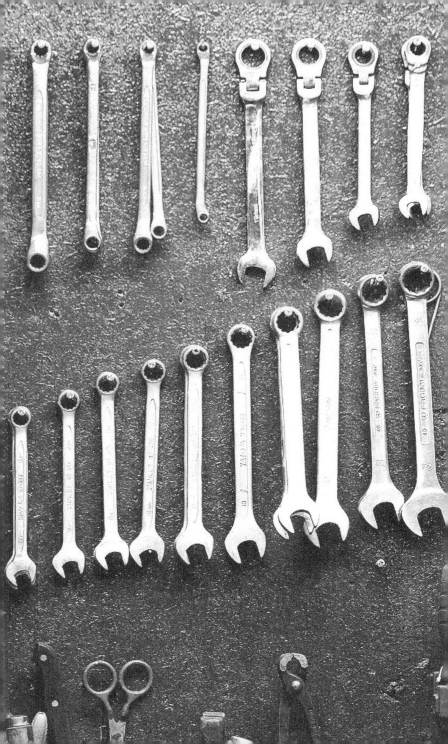

5 SPEAKING IN TONGUES IS A POTENT TRANSFORMATION TOOL.

SPEAKING IN TONGUES has profound benefits that will help us to transition from a life in the natural to the supernatural dimension of the Holy Spirit.

[1 Corinthians 14:2]

FOR HE THAT SPEAKETH IN AN UNKNOWN TONGUE speaketh not unto men, but unto God: for no man understandeth him; howbeit IN THE SPIRIT HE SPEAKETH mysteries.

When we speak in tongues, we place ourselves in the spirit through an act of our will. This is why speaking in tongues is also a potent transformation tool.

When we speak in tongues, we speak 'in the spirit. So when we speak in tongues, we activate ourselves in the spirit realm. We become more attuned to the Holy Spirit. Because our mind needs to step aside and let the spirit take over.

When we speak in tongues, we speak mysteries in the spirit. This means that speaking in tongues is also related to receiving revelation knowledge. When we speak in tongues, we keep growing in revelation knowledge. That is why Paul, who spoke more in tongues than others, [1 Corinthians 14:18] had the most revelation knowledge of all apostles.

When we speak in tongues, we speak to God about what is troubling us in our hearts, and in response, the Holy Spirit prays perfect prayers through us.

[Romans 8:26-28]

26 LIKEWISE THE SPIRIT ALSO HELPETH OUR INFIRMITIES: FOR WE KNOW NOT WHAT WE SHOULD PRAY FOR AS WE OUGHT: BUT THE SPIRIT ITSELF MAKETH INTERCESSION FOR US WITH GROANINGS WHICH CANNOT BE UTTERED.

27 AND HE THAT SEARCHETH THE HEARTS KNOWETH WHAT IS THE MIND OF THE SPIRIT, BECAUSE HE MAKETH INTERCESSION FOR THE SAINTS ACCORDING TO THE WILL OF GOD.

28 And we know that all things work together for good to them that love God, to them who are the called according to his purpose.

Speaking in tongues activates a part of the brain that is not connected to speech production. Dr. Andrew Newberg from the University of Pennsylvania did a study examining what is going on in the brains of people when they speak in tongues and in an understandable prayer language. He discovered that when people pray in an understandable language, the parts of the brain that have to do with speech production are activated, as can be expected. But, interestingly, when people speak in tongues, a part of the brain is activated that has nothing to do with speech production. See *Speaking in Tongues Medical Study proves Holy Spirit praying YouTube1*, https://www.youtube.com/watch?v=w20vRF3ikEA

This confirms the Scripture that also tells us that when we speak in tongues, our mind is not involved since we don't understand what we are saying but that we speaking 'in the spirit.'

[1 Corinthians 14:2]

For he that speaketh in an unknown tongue speaketh not unto men, but unto God: for NO MAN UNDERSTANDETH HIM; HOWBEIT IN THE SPIRIT HE SPEAKETH mysteries.

Moreover, **when we speak in tongues, it helps us to win in the spiritual war.**

[Ephesians 6:10-20]

10 Finally, my brethren, be strong in the Lord, and in the power of his might.

11 Put on the whole armour of God, that ye may be able to stand against the wiles of the devil.

12 For we wrestle not against flesh and blood, but against principalities, against powers, against the rulers of the darkness of this world, against spiritual wickedness in high places.

13 Wherefore take unto you the whole armour of God, that ye may be able to withstand in the evil day, and having done all, to stand.

14 Stand therefore, having your loins girt about with truth, and having on the breastplate of righteousness;

15 And your feet shod with the preparation of the gospel of peace;

16 Above all, taking the shield of faith, wherewith ye shall be able to quench all the fiery darts of the wicked.

17 And take the helmet of salvation, and the sword of the Spirit, which is the word of God:

18 PRAYING ALWAYS WITH ALL PRAYER AND supplication in the Spirit, and watching thereunto with all perseverance and supplication for all saints;

19 And for me, that utterance may be given unto me, that I may open my mouth boldly, to make known the mystery of the gospel,

20 For which I am an ambassador in bonds: that therein I may speak boldly, as I ought to speak.

Besides, **when we speak in tongues, we build ourselves up on our most holy faith.**

[Jude 17-21]

17 But, beloved, remember ye the words which were spoken before of the apostles of our Lord Jesus Christ;

18 How that they told you there should be mockers in the last time, who should walk after their own ungodly lusts.

19 These be they who separate themselves, sensual, having not the Spirit.

20 But ye, beloved, BUILDING UP YOURSELVES ON YOUR MOST HOLY FAITH, PRAYING IN THE HOLY [SPIRIT],

21 Keep yourselves in the love of God, looking for the mercy of our Lord Jesus Christ unto eternal life.

PART 3: SPEAKING IN TONGUES IS FOR ALL—YES, YOU TOO!

6 ALL THE FIRST BELIEVERS ON THE DAY OF PENTECOST SPOKE IN TONGUES.

THE CHURCH burst onto the scene on the day of Pentecost with a bang.

The disciples were all filled with liquid fire from above: Holy Spirit fire.

And they spoke in tongues.

All.

All 120 of them.

[Acts 2:1-4]

1And when the day of Pentecost was fully come, they were all with one accord in one place.

2 And suddenly there came a sound from heaven as of a rushing mighty wind, and it filled all the house where they were sitting.

3 3 And there appeared unto them cloven tongues like as of fire, and it sat upon each of them.

4 And THEY WERE ALL FILLED WITH THE HOLY [SPIRIT], AND BEGAN TO SPEAK WITH OTHER TONGUES, as the Spirit gave them utterance.

7 ALL THE FIRST NON-JEWS WHO RECEIVED THE GOSPEL SPOKE IN TONGUES.

PETER was the first person to preach the gospel to non-Jews—to the household of the Roman centurion, Cornelius.

Then, when Peter preached, the Holy Spirit fell on all who heard Peter's word.

All received the Holy Spirit and spoke in tongues.

[Acts 10:44-45]

44 While Peter yet spake these words, THE HOLY [SPIRIT] FELL ON ALL THEM WHICH HEARD THE WORD.
45 And they of the circumcision which believed were astonished, as many as

came with Peter, because that on the Gentiles also was poured out the gift of the Holy [Spirit].

But how did they know? It says in the next verse,

[Acts 10:44-45]

46 FOR THEY HEARD THEM SPEAK WITH TONGUES, and magnify God.

All the first disciples knew that receiving the Holy Spirit and speaking in tongues go together.

And they understood that when people hear the gospel, they ought to receive it by getting baptized.

Believing and getting baptized also go together.

According to Jesus in Mark 16:

[Mark 16:15-16]

... Go ye into all the world, and preach the gospel to every creature. 16 He that BELIEVETH AND IS BAPTIZED shall be saved ...

That is why in Acts, we always that when people believe the gospel, they get baptized.

Like in Acts 8, for example.

> [Acts 8:12]
>
> **But WHEN THEY BELIEVED Philip preaching the things concerning the kingdom of God, and the name of Jesus Christ, THEY WERE BAPTIZED, BOTH MEN AND WOMEN.**

All the early believers clearly understood this. So that is why in Acts 10, Peter then says,

> [Acts 10:47-48]
>
> **47 Can any man forbid water, that these should not be baptized, which have received the Holy [Spirit] as well as we?**
>
> **48 And he commanded them to be baptized in the name of the Lord. ...**

Take note: Peter says,

> [Acts 10:47]
>
> **... these ... HAVE RECEIVED THE HOLY [SPIRIT] AS WELL AS WE?**

The first non-Jewish disciples received the Holy Spirit like the first Jewish believers on the day of Pentecost.

Like the first believers on the day of Pentecost, they also *all* spoke in tongues.

55

8 ALL THE EPHESIANS RECEIVED THE HOLY SPIRIT AND SPOKE IN TONGUES AFTER THEY MET PAUL.

BEFORE PAUL came to them, the Ephesians were not yet converted.

They had not heard the gospel **yet**.

They heard the gospel from Paul. See Ephesians 1:13

Then they trusted in Christ.

They believed and got baptized.

[Acts 19:5]

When they heard this, they were baptized in the name of the Lord Jesus.

And then they received the Holy Spirit.

And also spoke in tongues.

All twelve.

We read,

[Acts 19:6]

And when Paul had laid his hands upon them, the Holy [Spirit] came on them; and THEY SPAKE WITH TONGUES, and prophesied.

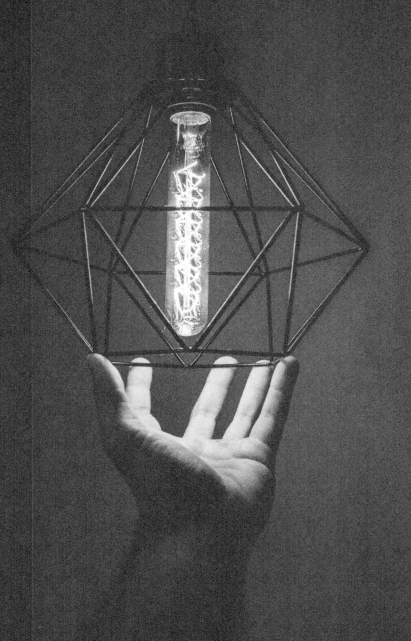

9 PAUL INSTRUCTED ALL THE EPHESIANS TO SPEAK IN TONGUES.

IN HIS LETTER to the Ephesians, Paul also talks about praying in tongues.

He instructs them in the context of spiritual warfare to be

[Ephesians 6:18]

PRAYING always with all prayer and supplication IN THE SPIRIT, and watching thereunto with all perseverance and supplication for all saints ...

Would the Ephesians have understood what Paul was talking about?

Certainly.

Because Paul established them in the gospel.

We read about this in Acts 19.

And it came to pass, that, while Apollos was at Corinth, Paul having passed through the upper coasts came to Ephesus: and finding certain disciples,

2 He said unto them, HAVE YE RECEIVED THE HOLY GHOST SINCE YE BELIEVED? And they said unto him, We have not so much as heard whether there be any Holy Ghost.

3 And he said unto them, Unto what then were ye baptized? And they said, Unto John's baptism.

4 Then said Paul, John verily baptized with the baptism of repentance, saying unto the people, that they should believe on him which should come after him, that is, on Christ Jesus.

5 When they heard this, they were baptized in the name of the Lord Jesus.

6 And WHEN PAUL HAD LAID HIS HANDS UPON THEM, THE HOLY GHOST CAME ON THEM; AND THEY SPAKE WITH TONGUES, and prophesied.

7 And all the men were about twelve.

These Ephesians didn't have the Holy Spirit yet when Paul met them.

So he needed to preach to them.

And then baptize them unto the name of Jesus.

And then, when he laid hands on them, they received the Holy Spirit.

And also spoke in tongues.

So, of course, the Ephesians clearly understood what Paul was talking about when he talked about praying in tongues.

10 ALL THE CHURCHES THAT PAUL ESTABLISHED SPOKE IN TONGUES.

PAUL WAS an apostle.

He helped believers to experience a true conversion.

So he helped them also to receive the Holy Spirit.

Like in the case of the Ephesians.

So, in all churches that Paul established, all believers had received the Holy Spirit and also spoke in tongues.

So when Paul wrote to them about speaking in tongues, they understood what he was talking about.

For example, when Paul wrote to the Corinthians, he said,

> [I Corinthians 14:18]
>
> *I thank my God, I SPEAK WITH TONGUES MORE THAN YE ALL ...*

Does this mean that all Corinthians spoke in tongues (for self-edification)?

Yes, certainly.

That's what Jesus said in Mark 16:

> [Mark 16:17]
>
> *And these SIGNS SHALL FOLLOW them that believe ... THEY SHALL SPEAK WITH NEW TONGUES ...*

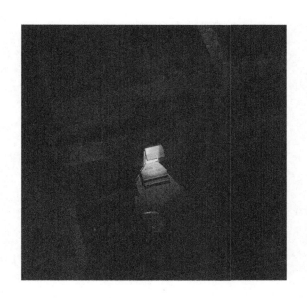

11 JUDE SAID THAT ALL BELIEVERS WHO HAVE THE SPIRIT SHOULD KEEP SPEAKING IN TONGUES.

WHEN WE pray with tongues, we build ourselves up.

This is what Jude tells us.

He says,

[Jude 17-21]

17 But, beloved, remember ye the words which were spoken before of the apostles of our Lord Jesus Christ;

18 How that they told you there should be mockers in the last time, who should walk after their own ungodly lusts.

19 These be they who separate themselves, sensual, having not the Spirit.

20 BUT YE, beloved, building up yourselves on your most holy faith, PRAYING IN THE HOLY [SPIRIT],

21 Keep yourselves in the love of God, looking for the mercy of our Lord Jesus Christ unto eternal life.

Would all the Spirit-filled believers who read Jude's letter have understood what Jude was talking about?

Yes, certainly.

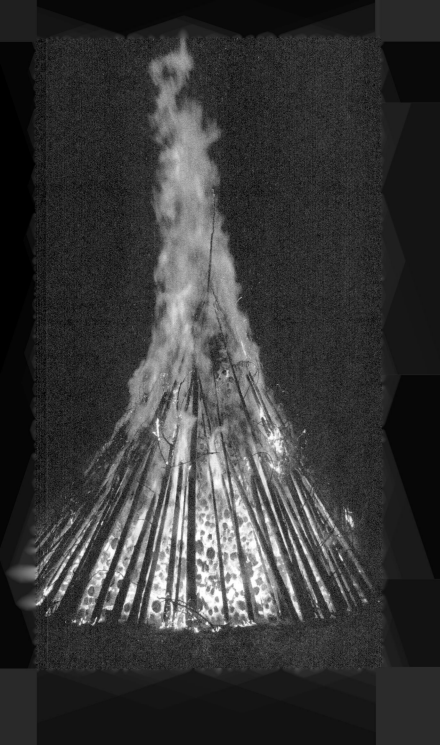

PART 4:
KEEP SPEAKING
IN TONGUES

12 WHAT IS THE CONCLUSION THEN?

KEEP SPEAKING in tongues—like Paul, the apostle.

Paul said to the Corinthians,

[1 Corinthians 14:18]

I thank my God, I SPEAK WITH TONGUES MORE THAN YE ALL ...

Paul knew about the transformative power of tongues.

So keep speaking in tongues.

Keep singing in tongues.

Do both, like Paul.

He says to the Corinthians,

[1 Corinthians 14:15]

... I will PRAY WITH THE SPIRIT, and I will pray with the understanding also. I will SING WITH THE SPIRIT, and I will sing with the understanding also.

So pray and sing in tongues.

And pray and sing in understanding.

13 OF COURSE, WE NEED TO BE WISE WHEN AND HOW WE PRAY IN TONGUES.

OF COURSE, we should employ common sense when, where, and how we pray in tongues.

We can pray in tongues at all times whenever we want to.

But it is wise to do it so that people who do not know what it is will not be taken aback by it.

In other words, we need to walk in love.

For example, Paul says that if a group of believers is together and those uninformed or pre-believing walk in, we need to be concerned about them.

If we are not catering to them, and we speak in tongues in a way that may shock them, they might think that we are mad.

Paul instructs the Corinthians in this matter.

Paul says,

[1 Corinthians 14:23-25]

23 IF THEREFORE THE WHOLE CHURCH BE COME TOGETHER INTO ONE PLACE, AND ALL SPEAK WITH TONGUES, AND THERE COME IN THOSE THAT ARE UNLEARNED, OR UNBELIEVERS, WILL THEY NOT SAY THAT YE ARE MAD?

24 But if all prophesy, and there come in one that believeth not, or one unlearned, he is convinced of all, he is judged of all:

25 And thus are the secrets of his heart made manifest; and so falling down on his face he will worship God, and report that God is in you of a truth.

If we are by ourselves, we can speak in tongues in any way we want to.

Quietly.

Or at the top of our voices.

As we feel led by the Spirit.

So, if we want to speak in tongues loudly, we need to find a place to do that without disturbing anyone.

It can be somewhere in the forest, a closed room, or a prayer closet.

But if we are in public, we need to be wise.

We can still pray in tongues, but we can do it quietly.

You may be married, and your spouse may sleep nicely next to you.

It may be at night or in the early hours of the morning, and the Lord wakes you up, and you have the urge to pray with tongues.

You can still do so.

But then do it quietly so that you don't disturb your sleeping spouse.

You can pray in tongues in public places.

For example, while walking on the street or sitting on a bus or train.

But again, you need to be concerned about the people around you.

This is common sense.

PART 5: WHAT IF I DON'T SPEAK IN TONGUES YET?

14 BEGIN WITH JESUS.

YOU CAN receive the Holy Spirit and speak in tongues today for one reason only.

It's because Jesus paid the price for it on the cross already.

This is the bottom line.

This is what we call the good news (the gospel).

So today, Jesus invites us to come into His Kingdom through what He has done for us on the cross.

15 THE GLORIOUS GOOD NEWS OF THE KINGDOM.

IN THE BEGINNING

BECAUSE OF ADAM

BECAUSE OF JESUS

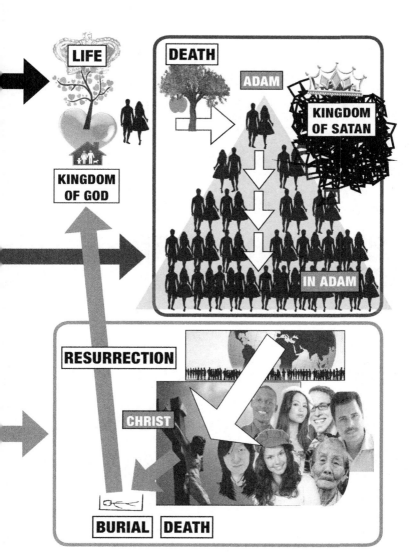

From Water Baptism 101: Everything You Need to Know About Getting Baptized by Albert Elisha & Peninnah Oberdorfer, pg. 34-35

16 I BELIEVE THE GOSPEL.

**JESUS DIED,
JESUS WAS BURIED,
JESUS WAS RAISED
FROM THE DEAD,
FOR ME.   SO**

~~JESUS~~ I DIED,
~~JESUS~~ I WAS BURIED,
~~JESUS~~ I WAS RAISED
FROM THE DEAD,
WITH HIM.

I RECEIVE THE GOSPEL.

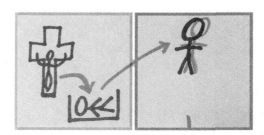

WHEN I BELIEVE

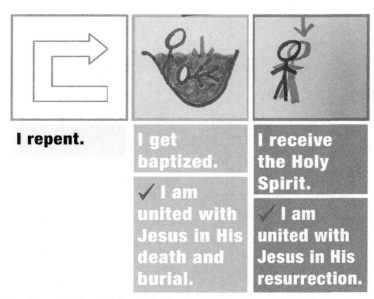

I repent.

I get baptized.

✓ **I am united with Jesus in His death and burial.**

I receive the Holy Spirit.

✓ **I am united with Jesus in His resurrection.**

From Water Baptism 101: Everything You Need to Know About Getting Baptized
by Albert Elisha & Peninnah Oberdorfer, pg. 43-42

17 WHAT SHALL WE DO?

REPENT.

BE BAPTIZED *every one of* *you* **IN THE NAME OF JESUS CHRIST FOR THE REMISSION OF SINS.**

And ye shall **RECEIVE THE GIFT OF THE HOLY SPIRIT.** ACTS 2:38

From Water Baptism 101: Everything You Need to Know About Getting Baptized by Albert Elisha & Peninnah Oberdorfer, pg. 40-41

18 PRACTICAL TIPS IN GENERAL.

#1 Get into the mindset of receiving.

The Holy Spirit is a gift.

Is it easy or difficult to receive a gift?

It's easy, right?

On the day of Pentecost, Peter instructed his listeners on what to do.

They had asked him, "What shall we do?"

[Acts 2:38-39]

38 Then Peter said unto them, Repent, and be baptized every one of you in the name of Jesus Christ for the remission of sins, and YE SHALL RECEIVE THE GIFT OF THE HOLY GHOST.

39 For the promise [of the Holy Spirit] is unto you, and to your children, and to all that are afar off, even as many as the Lord our God shall call.

From this, we can see that 1) the Holy Spirit is a gift, and 2) we can receive the Holy Spirit still today (because the promise is for all that are afar off). We are 2000 years afar of from the first time the Holy Spirit was given. But the promise that we would receive the gift of the Holy Spirit is still for us today.

So, you can be confident that you will receive the gift of the Holy Spirit.

And when you receive the Holy Spirit, you will also get to speak in tongues (as an accompanying sign). We will get to that very shortly.

But first, let's take a step back.

#2 Examine yourself: Have you understood, and do you believe the gospel of the Kingdom?

This is important.

If you have not heard the gospel of Jesus and what he has done for you yet, ask someone to explain it to you. See pages 84-89

Hear the gospel from someone who has already received the Holy Spirit and speaks in tongues. This will then impart faith to you.And when you believe, then you can receive easily.

#3 Examine yourself: Have you repented and been baptized in the name of Jesus Christ for the remission of sins?

This is what we see in the book of

[Acts 2:38-39]

38 Then Peter said unto them, REPENT, AND BE BAPTIZED EVERY ONE OF YOU IN THE NAME OF JESUS CHRIST FOR THE REMISSION OF SINS, and ye shall receive the gift of the Holy Ghost.

39 For the promise [of the Holy Spirit] is unto you, and to your children, and to all that are afar off, even as many as the Lord our God shall call.

Acts.

When people believed the gospel of the Kingdom of God and what Jesus did for them on the cross, they got baptized.

The word 'baptize' (baptizó) means to dunk.

IN ACTS, WHENEVER LISTENERS BELIEVED THE GOSPEL OF THE KINGDOM OF GOD AND THE NAME OF JESUS CHRIST, THEY GOT BAPTIZED IN WATER.

This is simple scripture.

From Water Baptism 101: Everything You Need to Know About Getting Baptized
by Albert Elisha & Peninnah Oberdorfer, pg. 58-59.

*T*HEN *those who gladly received his word were baptized.* Acts 2:41

But when they believed Philip preaching the things concerning the kingdom of God, and the name of Jesus Christ, they were baptized, both men and women. Acts 8:12

And he commanded the chariot to stand still: and they went down both into the water, both Philip and the eunuch; and he baptized him. Acts 8:38

And immediately there fell from his eyes as it had been scales: and he received sight forthwith, and arose, and was baptized. Acts 9:18

And he commanded them to be baptized in the name of the Lord. Acts 10:48

And when she was baptized, and her household, she besought us, saying, If ye have judged me to be faithful to the Lord, come into my house, and abide there. And she constrained us. Acts 16:15

And he took them the same hour of the night and washed their stripes. And immediately he and all his family were baptized. Acts 16:33

And Crispus, the chief ruler of the synagogue, believed on the Lord with all his house; and many of the Corinthians hearing believed, and were baptized. Acts 18:8

5 When they heard this, they were baptized in the name of the Lord Jesus. Acts 19:5

So, if you have been 'baptized' by sprinkling, get baptized by full immersion.

If you have been 'baptized,' as a baby (or when you didn't understand the gospel), get baptized again (since you now believe).

We find a case of this in the Bible in Acts 19.

Paul met some disciples (= 'taught ones') in Ephesus.

[Acts 19:1-6]

1 And it came to pass, that, while Apollos was at Corinth, Paul having passed through the upper coasts came to Ephesus: and finding certain disciples,

2 He said unto them, HAVE YE RECEIVED THE HOLY [SPIRIT] SINCE YE BELIEVED? And they said unto him, We have not so much as heard whether there be any Holy Ghost.

3 And he said unto them, UNTO WHAT THEN WERE YE BAPTIZED? And they said, Unto John's baptism.

4 Then said Paul, John verily baptized with the baptism of repentance, saying unto the people, that they should believe on him which should come after him, that is, on Christ Jesus.

5 WHEN THEY HEARD THIS, THEY WERE BAPTIZED IN THE NAME OF THE LORD JESUS.

6 And WHEN PAUL HAD LAID HIS HANDS UPON THEM, THE HOLY [SPIRIT] CAME ON THEM; AND THEY SPAKE WITH TONGUES, and prophesied.

So when Paul came to them, he asked them, *Have ye received the Holy Ghost since ye believed?*

But they had not yet. They didn't even know there was a Holy Spirit that they could receive.

This shows that they had not heard the full gospel yet. Because if people have heard the gospel, they will also have heard that they can receive the gift of the Holy Spirit through Jesus.

So Paul then went a step back.

He asked them, *Unto what then were ye baptized?*

And then Paul found out they had not yet been baptized in the name of the Lord Jesus.

They had been baptized unto John's

baptism. But John's baptism was not a baptism unto Jesus Christ yet.

When we get baptized in the name of Jesus Christ, we get baptized unto the death of Jesus.

In Romans 6, Paul explains this.

He says,

Jesus died for us on the cross.

And we died with Him.

[Romans 6:3-4]

3 Know ye not, that so many of us as were baptized into Jesus Christ were BAPTIZED INTO HIS DEATH?

4 Therefore we are BURIED WITH HIM BY BAPTISM INTO DEATH ...

Because He didn't die for himself.

He died for us.

More than that—He died *as* us!

So we get baptized in the name of Jesus Christ because we believe this.

Jesus' death was our death.

So that Jesus' resurrection becomes our resurrection.

So that we then can then receive the gift of the Holy Spirit!

Freely!

So this is what we see in the case of the Ephesians

We read,

#3 Have someone who

5 WHEN THEY HEARD THIS, THEY WERE BAPTIZED IN THE NAME OF THE LORD JESUS.

6 And WHEN PAUL HAD LAID HIS HANDS UPON THEM, THE HOLY GHOST CAME ON THEM; AND THEY SPAKE WITH TONGUES, and prophesied.

has already received the Holy Spirit and speaks in tongues lay hands on you and pray with you.

19 PRACTICAL TIPS THAT WILL HELP YOU SPEAK IN TONGUES.

Over the years, I've had the privilege to help many hundreds of believers receive the Holy Spirit and speak in tongues.

I have found the following insights from Billy Smith's book '*The Holy Spirit and His Gifts*' [1] extremely useful.

How can I allow the Holy Spirit to speak through me?

First, we must recognize ... that the Holy Spirit is a gift. Because it is a gift, God will not force anything on you. He will not force you to accept the Holy Spirit, and He will not force you to use the Holy Spirit by making you pray in tongues.

[Romans 6:13]

Yield yourselves unto God, as those

that are alive from the dead, AND
YOUR MEMBERS AS INSTRUMENTS
OF RIGHTEOUSNESS UNTO GOD.

There is a lot of difference between you
yielding yourself and your members to
God and God just taking possession.
You must also realize that when you
yield yourself to do something, you are
still in control. It is the same with the
Holy Spirit; we are in control of its use
...

When I pray in tongues, I am doing the
praying. I am yielding myself to the
Spirit of God. I am doing the speaking
with my tongue, but the Holy Spirit
is giving the utterance that I speak.
Notice what Paul says,

[I Corinthians 14:15]

I shall pray with the spirit and I shall
pray with the mind also; I shall sing
with the spirit and I shall sing with the
mind also.

Mark 16:17 (speaking about believers):

[Mark 16:17]

THEY WILL speak with new tongues.

You have a part in receiving the Holy
Spirit with evidence of speaking in

tongues. Your part is to release your faith in God's word that says if we ask the Father for the Holy Spirit, He will give [him] to us (see Luke 11:13). If we release faith, then that means we must act on our faith and speak out the sounds that the Holy Spirit gives to us.

Even so faith, if it has no works, is dead, being by itself. But someone may well say "You have faith, and I have works; show me your faith without the works, and I will show you my faith by my works.

I have prayed for thousands of believers to receive the Holy Spirit with the evidence of speaking in tongues. I can say that I have never had anyone who would obey the instructions that I am sharing with you, who did not have their prayer language manifested.

1. Trust God not to give you a bad gift of one that will harm you.

Every good thing bestowed and every perfect gift is from above, coming down from the Father of lights, with whom there is no variation, or shifting

shadow.

2. Ask according to Luke 11:13.

[Luke 11:13]

"If you then, being evil, know how to give good gifts to your children, how much more shall your heavenly Father give the Holy Spirit to those who ask Him?"

3. Then, by an act of your faith, speak the first sound. Do not speak a known language or a sound known to you. If you will make the first sound, God will continue speaking because faith moves God.

Many people want to start speaking in their own language, thinking God will make them change languages. This will not happen. You can speak only one language at a time, so you speak either in tongues or in your prayer language.

4. This is the point at which the sounds of your new prayer language will begin, but this is also the point at which your mind and the devil will begin to fight you.

a. The first thought that comes is, "Where is this coming from? Am I making this up?"

b. At this point, most people stop praying in this new language. But don't stop.

c. If other people are praying, they notice that they don't sound like everyone else, so they stop. But don't stop.

I have prayed for 50 or 60 people at one time, and none of them spoke in the same language. God has many different languages.

d. By this time, you should notice that these sounds are not coming from your head because your mind is thinking all kinds of thoughts at the same time you are praying.

e. Next, I encourage people to sing in tongues. Most of the time, they try to tell me they don't know how to sing in the Spirit. I tell them that the words they speak in their natural language are the same words they use when they sing in their natural language. Now use the same words you are speaking in tongues with and let God put a tune with it.

f. I want people to be very sure of their experience with the Holy Spirit, so I have them stop and start praying in tongues several times. I do this until they feel comfortable praying in tongues.

g. Next, I remind them that the Bible says that the devil is a liar and the father of lies. I tell them this because he will tell them every lie he can think of to keep them from continuing in the development of their prayer life. He does not want them to be praying the will of God for their lives.

h. Last of all, I remind them that Jude 20 says if they pray in tongues, they will be built up and edified. That leaves us with the thought that if you don't pray in tongues, you will not be built up and edified.

ABOUT THE AUTHOR

ALBERT ELISHA is a spiritual obstetrician. His calling is to help people experience a true spiritual birth into the Kingdom of God, including repentance, water baptism, and baptism with the Holy Spirit and fire.

Albert Elisha Oberdorfer, Mag. Phil., is a graduate of the IRIS Theological College in Pemba, Mozambique (Harvest School). He came to the Lord 30+ years ago when Jesus spoke to him in an audible voice. He currently lives in Thailand with his beautiful wife Prof. Peninnah Oberdorfer, M.D., PhD where they are stewarding a local Kingdom Family discipleship multiplication movement. He is also the author and co-author of more than 20 books covering the topics of the baptism of the Holy Spirit, water baptism, Kingdom culture and others including 'Only Jesus,' 'Holy Spirit Accountant,' 'A Flame for Every Head,' 'Do All Speak in Tongues?' and others.

REQUEST!

Dear reader, thank you for reading my book!

I'd really appreciate all of your feedback, and I love hearing what you have to say.

I'd appreciate your help to make the next edition of this book and my future books better.

Please feel free to kindly leave a helpful review on Amazon, letting me know what you thought of the book.

Thank you so much!

- Albert Elisha Oberdorfer

OTHER POPULAR BOOKS BY ALBERT ELISHA & PENINNAH OBERDORFER

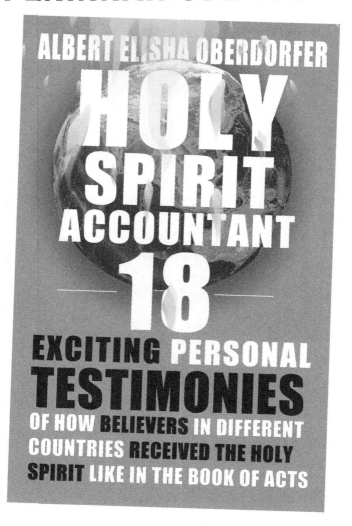

The amazing book of Acts is still being written today. In Acts, we read about people powerfully receiving the Holy Spirit and speaking in tongues. **This is still happening today all around the globe.**

This book details 18 compelling personal testimonies from the author.

- How a Baptist pastor in an Australian outback town finally receives the Holy Spirit and speaks in tongues after having been in ministry for more than 25 years,

- How a lady with a Muslim husband receives the Holy Spirit after first having had difficulties receiving the Holy Spirit in Manado on Sulawesi Island in Indonesia,

- How a dedicated Buddhist monk who had been doing solitary meditation in caves in high places in Tibet is delivered from demons and then powerfully receives the Holy Spirit in Thailand,

- How a whole Presbyterian congregation receives the Holy Spirit in Chiang Mai, Thailand, and many others.

These testimonies will inspire you and lift your expectations. Perhaps you haven't received the Holy Spirit with the accompanying sign of speaking in other tongues yet. Take heart. The word testimony means 'to do again.' What Jesus has done for others, He will do for you.

BOOK LIST.

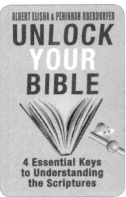

ALBERT ELISHA & PENINNAH OBERDORFER

UNLOCK YOUR BIBLE

4 Essential Keys to Understanding the Scriptures

ALBERT ELISHA & PENINNAH OBERDORFER

GOOD GOD

What Makes Us Change Our Minds About Jesus and Want to Follow Him

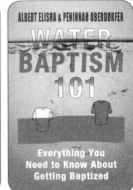

ALBERT ELISHA & PENINNAH OBERDORFER

WATER BAPTISM 101

Everything You Need to Know About Getting Baptized

ALBERT ELISHA & PENINNAH OBERDORFER

RECEIVE THE HOLY SPIRIT

—THE KINGDOM WAY

Like in the Book of Acts

ALBERT ELISHA & PENINNAH OBERDORFER

UNSHAKABLE

Building Kingdom Culture That Will Stand the Test of the End Times

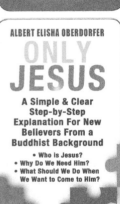

ALBERT ELISHA OBERDORFER

ONLY JESUS

A Simple & Clear Step-by-Step Explanation For New Believers From a Buddhist Background

• Who is Jesus?
• Why Do We Need Him?
• What Should We Do When We Want to Come to Him?

ALBERT ELISHA & PENINNAH OBERDORFER

LIT

How You Can Experience the Baptism With the Holy Spirit Today— as In the Book of Acts

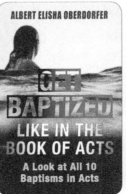

ALBERT ELISHA OBERDORFER

GET BAPTIZED LIKE IN THE BOOK OF ACTS

A Look at All 10 Baptisms in Acts

ALBERT ELISHA OBERDORFER

A BURIAL OF SELF

Why Baptism Is So Powerful

ALBERT ELISHA OBERDORFER

FLAME FOR EVERY HEAD

RECEIVE THE HOLY SPIRIT

TODAY —AS IN THE BOOK OF ACTS

ALBERT ELISHA OBERDORFER

HOLY SPIRIT ACCOUNTANT

18

EXCITING PERSONAL TESTIMONIES

OF HOW BELIEVERS IN DIFFERENT COUNTRIES RECEIVED THE HOLY SPIRIT LIKE IN THE BOOK OF ACTS

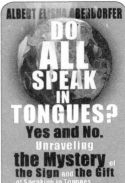

ALBERT ELISHA OBERDORFER

DO ALL SPEAK IN TONGUES?

Yes and No.

Unraveling the Mystery of the Sign and the Gift of Speaking in Tongues

ALBERT ELISHA OBERDORFER

I WISH I SPOKE IN TONGUES

How to Go From Wishing to Doing It

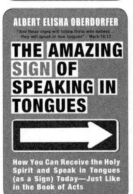

ALBERT ELISHA OBERDORFER

"And these signs will follow those who believe ... they will speak in new tongues" - Mark 16:17

THE AMAZING SIGN OF SPEAKING IN TONGUES

How You Can Receive the Holy Spirit and Speak in Tongues (as a Sign) Today—Just Like in the Book of Acts

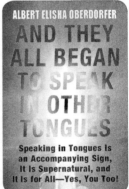

ALBERT ELISHA OBERDORFER

AND THEY ALL BEGAN TO SPEAK IN OTHER TONGUES

Speaking in Tongues Is an Accompanying Sign, It Is Supernatural, and It Is for All—Yes, You Too!

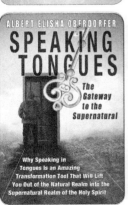

ALBERT ELISHA OBERDORFER

SPEAKING TONGUES

The Gateway to the Supernatural

Why Speaking in Tongues Is an Amazing Transformation Tool That Will Lift You Out of the Natural Realm into the Supernatural Realm of the Holy Spirit

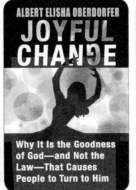

ALBERT ELISHA OBERDORFER

JOYFUL CHANGE

Why It Is the Goodness of God—and Not the Law—That Causes People to Turn to Him

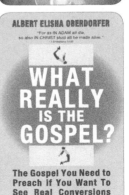

ALBERT ELISHA OBERDORFER

"For as IN ADAM all die, so also IN CHRIST shall all be made alive." - 1 Corinthians 15:22

WHAT REALLY IS THE GOSPEL?

The Gospel You Need to Preach if You Want To See Real Conversions

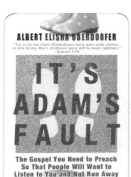

ALBERT ELISHA OBERDORFER

"For as by one man's disobedience many were made sinners, so also by one Man's obedience many will be made righteous." Romans 5:19

IT'S ADAM'S FAULT

The Gospel You Need to Preach So That People Will Want to Listen to You and Not Run Away

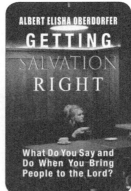

ALBERT ELISHA OBERDORFER

GETTING SALVATION RIGHT

What Do You Say and Do When You Bring People to the Lord?

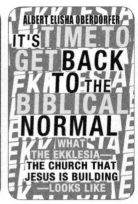

ALBERT ELISHA OBERDORFER

IT'S TIME TO GET BACK TO THE BIBLICAL NORMAL

WHAT THE EKKLESIA—
THE CHURCH THAT JESUS IS BUILDING
—LOOKS LIKE

ALBERT ELISHA & PENINNAH OBERDORFER

YOU HAVE HIS RIGHTEOUSNESS

How to Get Off the Hamster Wheel of Religion and Find True Rest for Your Soul

ALBERT ELISHA OBERDORFER

BEWARE OF DOGS!

An illustrated verse-by-verse commentary of Philippians 3

PAUL'S ASTONISHING REVELATION IN PHILIPPIANS 3 THAT WILL PROTECT YOUR SOUL

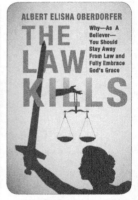

ALBERT ELISHA OBERDORFER

THE LAW KILLS

Why—As A Believer—You Should Stay Away From Law and Fully Embrace God's Grace

ALBERT ELISHA OBERDORFER

TRANSFORMATION THROUGH PAIN

How God Uses Your Setbacks and Sufferings to Transform You Into a Catalyst of Healing, Restoration, and Hope

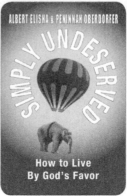

ALBERT ELISHA & PENINNAH OBERDORFER

SIMPLY UNDESERVED

How to Live By God's Favor

"I will say of the LORD, He is my refuge and my fortress: my God; in him will I trust." - Psalm 91:2

Speak the Word to Yourself— It Is Powerful

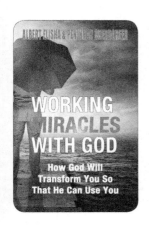

ALBERT ELISHA & PENINNAH MAGUGWANA

WORKING MIRACLES WITH GOD

How God Will
Transform You So
That He Can Use You

And They All Began to Speak in Tongues: Speaking in Tongues Is an Accompanying Sign, It Is Supernatural, and It Is for All—Yes, You Too!

Copyright 2021 © Albert L. Oberdorfer

ISBN 9798524290113

Unless otherwise quoted, all Scripture quotations are from the King James Version of the Bible.

PICTURE CREDITS

Unless otherwise stated, all images are courtesy of Pexels.com and Pixabay.com. The images on page 119 and on the cover are from the author. Any inadvertent omissions can be rectified in future editions.

ENDNOTES

1 Billy B. Smith, *The Holy Spirit and His Gifts,* Billy B. Smith Ministries Publications, pg. 44-49.

Printed in Great Britain
by Amazon